CONTENTS

▲ THEODORE ROOSEVELT stood still for this photo! It was taken in 1900.

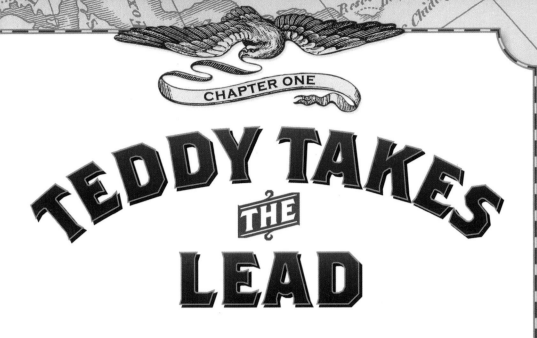

CHAPTER ONE

TEDDY TAKES THE LEAD

It was early winter and the evening was chilly. The president of the United States wanted to take a walk. He left the White House with a few friends.

The president was in the lead. The other men hurried to keep up. They chatted and joked. When the president laughed, his whole body shook. He threw back his head and flashed a mouth full of white teeth.

> *"When you play, play hard. When you work, don't play at all."*
>
> —THEODORE ROOSEVELT

The group stayed on a straight path. They never turned left or right. They climbed hills and pushed through bushes. Was there a puddle in the way? They splashed right through it. Straight on they went. Then they stopped at the wooded banks of the Potomac River.

Would the president turn back? No way! He began to undress. So did the others. They piled their clothes on the riverbank. Then one by one they jumped into the water and swam for the other side.

This may have been a strange way to act—but not for Theodore Roosevelt. He was the twenty-sixth president of the United States. And almost everything about him was unusual.

President Roosevelt—or "Teddy"—was full of energy. He didn't just hike. He boxed, wrestled, played tennis, and rode horses.

Teddy liked to keep busy. And he liked to get things done. Once he set a goal, he wouldn't let anything stand in his way. That's why he liked his "point-to-point" walks. He set out from one point and went straight to another point. He didn't let anything force him off his path—not even the Potomac River!

Good Timing

Teddy became president in 1901. He was the perfect man for the job—a new kind of president for a new century. He wanted to push the country in a different direction.

◀ TEDDY CHOPPED down trees and cleared land for exercise.

▲ HEADING WEST
As the U.S. grew, many people loaded up wagons and headed west. In 1800 there were sixteen states. By 1900 there were forty-five!

Times were changing. The U.S. continued to grow. Settlers kept moving farther west. The country's leaders worried about problems inside the U.S. The nation stayed out of world events.

Teddy wanted the U.S. to be a world leader. He wanted it to set big, important goals. Then he wanted the country to march toward its goals, no matter what. He saw the future of the country as if it were a giant point-to-point hike. And he was the man to lead.

How did Teddy get to be the way he was? Why did he make the choices he made? To find the answers, you have to go back to the time when Teddy was just beginning his life.

CHAPTER TWO

TEDDY'S BUSY BOYHOOD

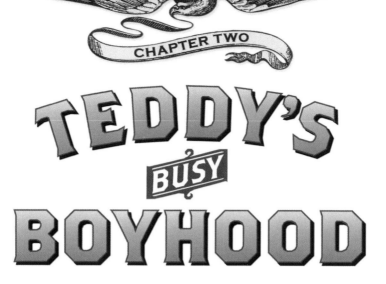

When Teddy was a little boy, his nickname was Teedie. (Later on people would call him Teddy. But he never liked that name.) Teedie lived in New York City. The Roosevelt family had lived there for hundreds of years.

▲ TEDDY'S FATHER, Theodore

Teedie's father was Theodore Roosevelt Sr. He had strong ideas about how people should act. He believed that everyone should work hard. He also believed he had a duty to help others, including those less fortunate.

Teedie's mother, Martha, was from Georgia. She was known for her great beauty and her

◄ WHEN HE was four years old, Teddy posed for this photo. Check out his clothes!

gentleness. She loved art and music. People called her by her nickname, Mittie.

Teedie was born on October 27, 1858. When he was two, a terrible war started in the U.S.— the Civil War. It was a war fought mostly between the northern and southern parts of the U.S.

Mittie was a southerner. Her brothers fought in the war on the side of the South. Teddy Sr. was a northerner. He believed in the cause of the North. What should he do? He knew it would hurt Mittie if he fought against the South. So Teddy Sr. did not go to war. Instead he paid another man to fight in his place. And he did work for the northern army that didn't involve fighting.

Teedie felt bad that his father

▲ TEDDY'S MOTHER, Martha

5

stayed out of the war. He thought fighting was a duty. Years later, in another war, Teedie would jump at the chance to fight. But first he had to grow up.

A Sickly Kid

Teedie had two sisters, Anna and Corinne. He also had a younger brother, Elliot. All the Roosevelt children had health problems. Teedie's were the worst.

He had bad stomach and head pains. He also had asthma. People with asthma have trouble getting enough oxygen into their lungs. Nowadays there are many medicines for people with asthma. But when Teddy was little, doctors couldn't do much to help.

Nights were especially hard for the young boy. When Teedie couldn't breathe, Teddy Sr. would take him for a fast carriage

▶ THE ROOSEVELTS had this picture taken when they visited Egypt in 1872. Teddy is the second child from the right.

ride. His father would hold him tight as the horses galloped through the dark, empty streets. These rides seemed to help his lungs fill with fresh air.

When Teedie was too sick to play, he sat and looked at books. Before he learned to read, he studied pictures. He loved looking at animals best.

When he wasn't sick, Teedie was full of energy! It was hard for him to sit still. During trips to the country, he spent all day outdoors. He rode horses, swam, and climbed trees. He was always moving.

TEEDIE'S HOME MUSEUM

Teedie set up a natural history museum at home. Wherever he went, he collected small animals such as frogs and turtles. He even learned how to use chemicals to preserve them. The chemicals smelled terrible. So did the dead animals! On family vacations Teedie's brother, Elliot, begged to have a separate bathroom. He didn't want to share a sink or bathtub with Teedie's creatures.

Animals Everywhere

Even in the city, Teedie spent most of his time outside. Often he searched for unusual bugs and animals. He was very interested in studying them. The house was filled with his creatures. He kept snakes in the water pitchers. He kept a snapping turtle in the washroom. Once he tipped his hat to a family friend on a streetcar. Out hopped two frogs! Imagine his friend's surprise!

Teedie was interested in everything about animals. He cut apart dead animals to study their bones. He wanted to know what they ate and how long they lived. He drew pictures of birds and insects and described everything he saw. He wanted to be a naturalist, someone who studies plants and animals.

As the years passed, Teedie's health did not improve. He was still weak and sick. When he was twelve, his father took him aside. "Theodore," he said. "You must make your body. It is hard [dull work] to make one's body, but I know you will do it."

The young boy took the challenge. "I'll make my body," he said. So his father built him a gym. Teedie exercised for several hours every day. He wanted to build up his chest and his arms. The hard work paid off. When he was ready for college, Teddy was strong and healthy.

► **TEDDY'S SIDEBURNS** were growing into a beard when he was seventeen.

CHAPTER THREE

TEDDY ENTERS POLITICS

Teddy entered Harvard University in 1876. He was a bundle of energy. He worked and played hard. He talked all the time. And he loved books. He could read very fast, and he had an amazing memory. Years later he could repeat things he'd read—word for word!

Teddy planned to be a scientist. But two things happened that would change his life forever.

During Teddy's second year at school,

▶ **WELCOME TO HARVARD!**
Harvard University is in Cambridge, Massachusetts. Teddy was happy there!

his father died suddenly. It was a shock. Teddy's friends and family worried about him. They were afraid he would never get over his sadness.

But Teddy was a man of action. He worked harder than ever to help take his mind off his troubles.

Early in his third year at Harvard, joy came back into his

▲ **READY TO RUN**
Teddy ran track in college. Here he is in his running gear.

life. He fell in love with a young woman named Alice Lee. Teddy and Alice planned to get married.

Alice made it clear that she did not want Teddy to become a scientist. She didn't like the idea of cutting up animals or the smell of the chemicals he used.

Teddy wanted to please Alice. He also wanted to honor his father. He could do that by working to make the world a better place. And if he were famous, that would

◀ **TEDDY GRADUATED** from Harvard University, where he studied science.

bring honor to the family name. He knew what he should do with his life. Instead of science he would go into politics!

Teddy the Lawmaker

By November 1881 Teddy was a married man. He was also an elected official. Teddy ran as a Republican candidate for the New York State Assembly, the lawmaking body of the state.

Teddy was different from most of the others in the assembly. He stood out for several reasons. There was the way he looked: Teddy had his hair parted down the middle. He wore an eyeglass that clipped to his nose and hung from a chain. He liked fancy clothes.

Teddy's background was different, too. His family was wealthy. He had traveled around the U.S. and even to Egypt. And he had a university education. Most people in politics at that time did not come from rich families. They did not have college degrees. So Teddy seemed out of place in the state government.

The other lawmakers soon found that Teddy was a hard worker. He worked to pass laws about who should get government jobs. Usually politicians would give jobs to people who helped them get elected. Teddy believed people should work in government only if they were good at their jobs.

The public liked Teddy. When he ran for office again in 1883, he got most of the votes.

Everything was going very well for the young lawmaker. Then in early 1884 tragedy struck.

▲ TEDDY (standing on the right) was proud of this photo taken with other lawmakers. He thought people should get government jobs based on their brains and not who they knew.

Teddy and Alice had been expecting a baby. On February 12 Alice Roosevelt had a little girl. The baby was named Alice after her mother. Teddy and his wife were thrilled!

The baby was healthy, but Teddy's wife became ill. At the same time Teddy's mother, Mittie, was also very sick. On February 14 Mittie died. A few hours later, in the same house, Teddy's wife died, too. On the same terrible day, Teddy lost his mother and his wife.

Teddy felt his world had ended. He did not know what to do. He turned to his sister Anna and asked her to take care of the new baby. Anna thought Teddy should build a home for his daughter.

Teddy owned a piece of land in New York on Long Island. He decided to build a large house there. He called his new home Sagamore Hill. (Sagamore was the name of a Native American chief. The chief had used the hill as a meeting place in the 1600s.)

Teddy finished his term in the New York State Assembly. Then he had to get away. He headed west, leaving Alice at home with Anna. Teddy had always loved the outdoors. Being active and busy in the outdoors would help the young widower forget his deep sadness.

▼ SAGAMORE HILL is in Oyster Bay, New York. Teddy loved the house and spent much time there.

▲ **TEDDY PROUDLY POSES** in his western gear! He even took off his glasses for the photo.

CHAPTER FOUR

COWBOY ON THE RANGE

Teddy moved to what is now North Dakota. The local people thought he was a pretty odd character. He talked like an Easterner. He seemed too small for the rugged western life. And sometimes he wore glasses! That was very unusual for a cowboy. Everyone thought Teddy would find life too hard out west.

But people would soon change their minds. Teddy rode out on the trail with a guide to hunt buffalo. The weather was cold and rainy. They couldn't find any buffalo. But Teddy never complained. In fact, he was having a wonderful time!

It took two weeks for Teddy to find a buffalo. After he shot it, he did a little dance around it. He sent the animal's head back east. He wanted to have it stuffed to hang on his wall.

A Conservationist Is Born

Teddy loved being in the wild country. No matter how tired, wet, or hungry he got, he stayed in a good mood. Teddy loved nature. He thought it was beautiful and amazing. He studied every new plant or animal to see what he could learn.

Teddy said a "hunter should be a lover of nature as well as of sport, or he will miss half the pleasure of being in the woods."

He realized that nature must be protected or it will disappear. People will tear it down or spoil it. People who try to protect nature are conservationists. One day Teddy would become the greatest conservationist president in history.

Teddy lived in the West for two years. When he headed back east, he was a changed man. He was tough and healthy. He would go back to politics, but his life in the West would always be part of him.

Teddy went home to Sagamore Hill. Now he could get to know his little daughter, Alice. He would also get to know an old friend again. Her name was Edith Carow.

Edith and Teddy had known each other as children. They met again after the death of Teddy's wife. Teddy and Edith got married at the end of 1886.

◀ **ON THE TRAIL** Teddy may have been happiest in the great outdoors. He's shown here with his horse Manitan.

MYSTERY PLACE

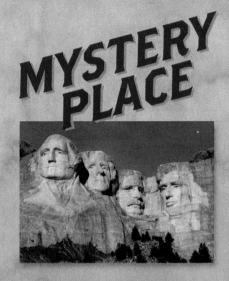

)☞**Clue 1:** You can find this mountain in Keystone, South Dakota.

)☞**Clue 2:** The four U.S. presidents carved into the mountain represent the first 150 years of U.S. history. They are George Washington, Thomas Jefferson, Theodore Roosevelt, and Abraham Lincoln. Each face is sixty feet tall.

)☞**Clue 3:** Sculptor Gutzon Borglum began drilling into the 5,725-foot mountain in 1927. It took fourteen years to finish.

Can you name this mountain?

The couple lived at Sagamore Hill with Teddy's daughter, Alice. Over the years Edith and Teddy had five more children: Theodore, Kermit, Ethel, Archibald, and Quentin.

Teddy spent much of his time writing. He had written part of his first book while he was still in college. Throughout his life he continued to write about history, nature, politics, and his own life. He wrote more than forty-five books. He could have been a writer and nothing else. But that was not enough for Teddy. He had too much energy for just one career. He needed much more to do to keep him busy and happy!

A New Job

Teddy became a police commissioner in New York City. At that time some of the police in New York were not honest. Some slept on the job instead of keeping the streets safe. Some would take money from criminals. In return the police promised not to arrest the lawbreakers.

Teddy walked through the streets late at night. He caught many police officers breaking the law. He made sure that anyone not doing his job would get in trouble.

All his life Teddy had believed that the problems of the poor were their own fault. But spending time in poor areas of New York City helped change his mind. Now he felt that the poor could not improve their lives if they were not paid fairly for their work. It made Teddy angry to see bosses get rich off the labor of the poor. It was a lesson that he would always remember and try to do something about later in his life.

▲ **AS HEAD** of the New York City police, Teddy made the city a safer place.

CHAPTER FIVE

TEDDY AND THE ROUGH RIDERS

In 1897 Teddy was named Assistant Secretary of the Navy by President William McKinley.

At about that time, trouble started brewing in Cuba—a small island in the Atlantic Ocean, ninety miles from Florida. In the 1890s Spain was in control of Cuba. Teddy thought Spain should leave the island. He wanted the U.S. to be the only powerful nation in this part of the world.

Most Cubans wanted Spain to leave, too. Some Cubans joined together to try to kick Spain out.

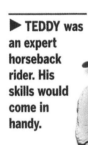

▶ TEDDY was an expert horseback rider. His skills would come in handy.

◄ IN 1898 TEDDY got ready to head for Cuba. There he led the Rough Riders.

CANADA

ME
VT
NH
NY MA
RI
CT
PA NJ
OH MD
DE
WV ★
Washington, D.C.
VA
NC
SC
GA Atlantic
Ocean
FL

Havana
★ CUBA

President McKinley tried to avoid war. But Teddy was eager for it. Why? He thought war would make Americans strong. He probably had another reason, too: Teddy felt bad that his father had not fought in the Civil War. He wanted to make up for that fact and honor his family. And he didn't want to miss out on what he thought would be a great adventure.

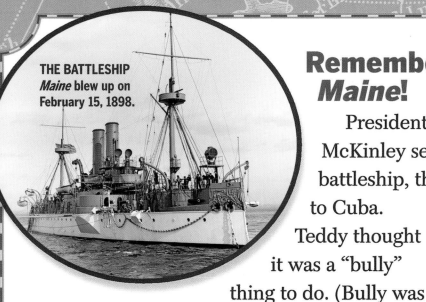

Remember the *Maine!*

President McKinley sent a battleship, the *Maine*, to Cuba.

Teddy thought it was a "bully" thing to do. (Bully was Teddy's word for "excellent.")

On the night of February 15, 1898, the *Maine* exploded. Two hundred sixty-six men were killed.

No one knew the cause of the explosion, but many blamed Spain. Some newspapers said the U.S. should go to war. They made up stories about the Spanish "attack." They knew that war would sell a lot of papers. (Experts now believe the explosion was an accident. Spain had nothing to do with it.)

Teddy was thrilled. He believed Spain had attacked the U.S. Now the U.S. could defend its honor.

Teddy formed a volunteer army of one thousand men. They were nicknamed Roosevelt's Rough Riders.

The men fought at a place called San Juan Hill. Many soldiers were seriously wounded, and eighty-nine died. Teddy was proud of his men and he was glad the U.S. won the battle. He said it was "the great day of my life."

ROUGH RIDERS proudly pose at the top of San Juan Hill after the battle. The U.S. won the Spanish-American War.

CHAPTER SIX

PRESIDENT FOR A "SQUARE DEAL"

Newspaper writers had always liked Teddy. He did so many unusual things that he often made news. The Spanish-American War added to Teddy's fame. He was a great hero. By the end of 1898, he had been elected

governor of New York.

Voters loved Teddy. Reporters loved to write about him. But Republican leaders weren't so sure they trusted him as governor. Teddy was too popular and hard to control. He did what he thought was right, not what the party leaders wanted him to do.

▲ TEDDY was photographed everywhere he went. He is shown here at a football game!

The leaders had an idea: In the next election, Teddy should be President McKinley's running mate for vice president. They thought he might listen more to Republican Party leaders as a vice president than he did as the governor of New York.

The McKinley/Roosevelt team won the election. They took office on March 4, 1901.

But the team didn't last too long. On September 6 President McKinley was shot. He died eight days later. Theodore Roosevelt became the president of the United States.

◀ WILLIAM McKINLEY (left) meets with his vice president, Theodore Roosevelt. A few months after this photo was taken, McKinley was assassinated.

▲ THE WHITE HOUSE became Roosevelt's home in September 1901.

Teddy was forty-two when he became the youngest U.S. president. As president he surprised everyone. He tried to make the country do what he thought it should. He used power in a new way.

First he went after the railroads. He wanted to make sure that they didn't join together to set high prices.

When companies compete for customers, prices go down. If companies agree not to compete, prices go up. That's a monopoly and it is against the law.

For years many businesses had ignored the law. Teddy changed that. He told business owners that they must not join together to keep prices high. They would have to compete against one another for customers or he would make sure they were brought to trial. He began with the railroads. But he didn't stop there. As president he used the law forty-five times.

> *"Far and away the best prize that life offers is the chance to work hard at work worth doing."*
>
> —THEODORE ROOSEVELT

Teddy used his power again to end a strike in the coal mines of Pennsylvania. Miners had stopped working because they wanted to be paid more and to

▲ TEDDY GIVES A SPEECH. The men in hats are newspaper reporters. Remember, this was before radio and television! It was also before there were many female reporters.

◀ **TEDDY** was always interested in helping to better the lives of children as well as adults.

work only eight hours a day. (The owners wanted them to work more hours.)

The mine owners said they would not talk to the miners. They would just wait until the strikers gave up. But winter was coming. Teddy knew that people needed coal to make heat. He said the owners had to talk to the miners. If they didn't, Teddy would bring in U.S. soldiers to work in the mines. The mines would run, but the owners wouldn't get paid. So the owners gave

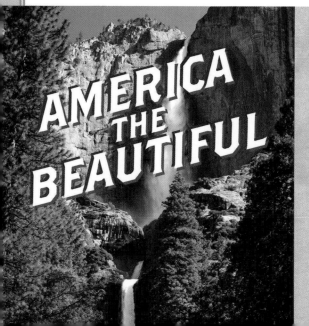

AMERICA THE BEAUTIFUL

If you should ever visit North Dakota, perhaps you will get to see Theodore Roosevelt National Park. The park was named in honor of the president because of his love of the outdoors and of nature. The park covers 70,447 acres in the wilderness of North Dakota. Today the park is part of the National Park System—a U.S. government agency that is part of the Department of the Interior.

in. The workers got better pay and an eight-hour day.

Teddy wasn't trying to favor the workers over the owners. He did what he thought was fair. He said all people should have a "square deal," a fair one.

Teddy's Great Plans

It's no surprise that Teddy also used his power to protect nature. As president he set aside about 230 million acres of land! From Puerto Rico to Alaska there are wild areas you can visit today because Teddy made them into parks a century ago.

Teddy had another great plan. He wanted to build a canal in Central America. In 1900 sailing from Florida to California took a very long time. Ships had to travel all the way around Central and South America. The trip was about fifteen thousand miles.

Yellowstone, which was opened in 1872, was the first national park in the world. The National Park System includes natural and historic sites spread across the U.S.

Today there is a national park in every state but Delaware. For a listing of national parks, visit the website at www.nps.gov.

▶ VISITING CALIFORNIA, Teddy Roosevelt is dwarfed by the giant sequoia trees.

Teddy wanted to build a shortcut. Panama was the best place for it. In Panama a very narrow strip of land separates the Atlantic and Pacific Oceans.

But there was a problem. Panama was part of another country, Colombia. Colombia didn't want the U.S. to build a canal. So the people of Panama decided to break away from Colombia. Teddy sent U.S. soldiers to help Panama fight. When Panama became a separate country, the U.S. could build the canal.

Work on the canal began in 1904. Teddy was re-elected as president the same year. In 1914 the first ship sailed through the canal. Now ships could move more quickly around the world. The canal helped the U.S. become a world power.

During his second term, Teddy kept up his conservation work. He helped make it illegal to sell food and drugs that were not pure

A MAN, A PLAN, A CANAL: PANAMA

The canal took ten years to build. In 1906 Teddy told canal workers, "This is one of the great works of the world. It is greater than you yourselves at the moment realize."

and clean. And in 1906 he won the Nobel Peace Prize, a very important award, for helping to end a war between Russia and Japan.

Teddy used the power of his office in a new way. He helped make laws that were fair for everyone. He pushed the country to act like a world power.

TEDDY AND THE BIG STICK

Teddy had a favorite saying based on an African proverb: "Speak softly and carry a big stick. You will go far." If you were strong—and willing to use your strength—people would listen to you. You didn't have to make threats. A strong country was one that could use force if it had to.

The Big Stick policy meant that Teddy could tell others what to do. This worked on U.S. business leaders and on leaders of other countries.

CHAPTER SEVEN

TEDDY AND THE BULL MOOSERS

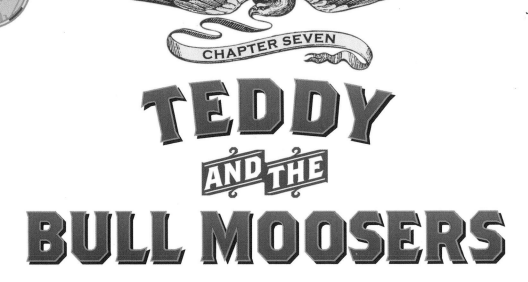

Teddy left the White House in 1909. He wondered what he should do with his life now. He was only fifty years old. He felt that was much too young to stop working and retire.

Teddy wanted to do something unusual. So he decided to go hunting in Africa, with his grown son Kermit. Teddy wrote about his trip for a magazine. And he took along three animal experts to ship back the animals he killed. Today the wild animals of Africa have been overhunted. Many of them are in danger of

◀ **ON THE ROAD TO AFRICA**
Teddy got to ride a camel during his trip!

▲ **TEDDY AND KERMIT** sit atop a water buffalo they killed on their trip to Africa. Back then no one thought about the possibility of animals dying out.

becoming extinct. It's against the law to kill most of them now. But in 1909 there were many more animals. No one thought it was wrong to hunt them.

Teddy and Kermit killed 512 animals. There were lions, elephants, zebras, and many more. The experts sent the animals to the Smithsonian Museum in Washington, D.C., and the American Museum of Natural History in New York City.

THIS IS A RECEIPT FOR ONE DOLLAR CONTRIBUTED TO THE CAMPAIGN FUND OF THE PROGRESSIVE PARTY.

Teddy Runs Again!

Teddy and Kermit headed home in June 1910. Teddy began making speeches all over the country for the Republican Party. He still had strong ideas about everything. Some of his ideas went against the Republicans' plan.

It was almost time for the next presidential election. Teddy decided to run again. But the Republicans did not want him to be their candidate. So Teddy ran on the smaller Progressive Party ticket.

At that time American women could not vote. Many children worked rather than going to school. People could be made to work long hours. The Progressives said that these things were wrong.

Teddy was feeling strong and in good health. He said he felt "as fit as a bull moose." People began to call his party the "Bull Moosers."

One night Teddy was on his way to make a speech in Milwaukee, Wisconsin, when a man shot him. Teddy would not go to a hospital. Instead he gave the speech with a bullet in his right lung. The crowd was amazed when they found out he was wounded. At the end of his talk, he went to the hospital. Doctors said it was safer to leave the bullet where it was than to operate.

Although Teddy was very popular, he lost the election. Woodrow Wilson, a Democrat, became the twenty-eighth president.

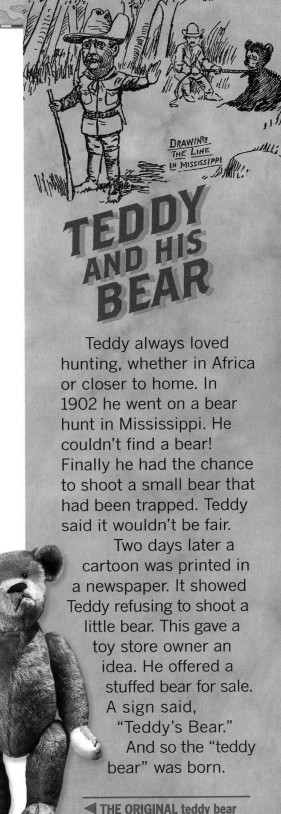

DRAWING THE LINE IN MISSISSIPPI

TEDDY AND HIS BEAR

Teddy always loved hunting, whether in Africa or closer to home. In 1902 he went on a bear hunt in Mississippi. He couldn't find a bear! Finally he had the chance to shoot a small bear that had been trapped. Teddy said it wouldn't be fair.

Two days later a cartoon was printed in a newspaper. It showed Teddy refusing to shoot a little bear. This gave a toy store owner an idea. He offered a stuffed bear for sale. A sign said, "Teddy's Bear." And so the "teddy bear" was born.

◄ THE ORIGINAL teddy bear

CHAPTER EIGHT

TEDDY— THE ONE AND ONLY

After the election Teddy took another trip with Kermit and a group of explorers. This time they went to South America. Teddy wanted to explore a river in Brazil called the River of Doubt. No one had mapped it yet.

It would be a dangerous trip, and Teddy was not healthy. He still had the bullet in his lung. His eyesight was failing. But his love of adventure won out. He said, "It's my last chance to be a boy again."

▶ THE RIVER OF DOUBT
A trip to Brazil provided a thrilling adventure for Teddy.

They headed for the rain forest. Once they began to explore the river, they had no idea where it would lead them. The river was full of rushing rapids. The forest was full of biting insects. Several people died on the trip. Teddy was almost one of them. He hurt his leg badly, and he caught a dangerous sickness.

Teddy knew that it would be hard for the others to take a sick man out of the jungle. He told his son to leave him behind. But Kermit refused. He and the others carried Teddy out of the jungle.

In the end, the trip was a success. Teddy and his group had completed the trip on the unexplored river.

Presidential Firsts

▲ TEDDY takes his first plane trip.

Theodore Roosevelt was the first president to:

- ☞ Fly in an airplane
- ☞ Own a car
- ☞ Use a typewriter
- ☞ Go in a submarine
- ☞ Travel outside the U.S. while president
- ☞ Use a camera
- ☞ Win a Nobel Prize
- ☞ Create national monuments
- ☞ Invite an African American to dine at the White House

(The government of Brazil renamed it Roosevelt River.) The explorers had brought back thousands of animals for scientists to study.

But at the end of the trip, Teddy was in very poor health. His leg never healed completely. The tropical fever that he caught in the jungle kept coming back.

Farewell, Teddy

In 1917 the U.S. entered World War I. Teddy wanted to do his part. But it was too late for him. There was nothing he could do to help out.

All of Teddy's sons went to fight. In 1918 his son Quentin was killed. Teddy was proud of his son, but his heart was broken.

The war ended in November 1918. Two months later, on January 6, 1919, Teddy died peacefully in his sleep. He was sixty years old.

Teddy had always loved life. To him it was an adventure. Teddy was brave and curious. He worked as hard as anyone could. He was a strong leader. He always did what he thought was right. Teddy loved the United States and was willing to die for it. And yet he always had the spirit and optimism of a young child.

The U.S. has had many colorful, inspiring, and wonderful leaders. But there has only been one like Theodore Roosevelt.

▲ IN 1917 TEDDY WAS THE STAR of a big parade in Chicago. He was honored for his explorations and for all his good works.

TALKING ABOUT TEDDY

▲ Charles Markis

TIME For Kids editor Kathryn Satterfield spoke with Charles Markis. He works at Sagamore Hill, which is run by the National Park Service.

Q: *Why should we be grateful to Theodore Roosevelt when we visit national parks?*

A: The idea of setting aside areas in nature was first suggested by Theodore Roosevelt. He set an example that was followed by every president since his time.

Q: *In the conservation world, what was Theodore Roosevelt's most important achievement?*

A: He set aside 230 million acres of land for national parks, wildlife lands, and forests. That's about the size of the states on the East Coast, from Maine to Florida.

VISITORS to California's Yosemite National Park can thank Teddy Roosevelt for starting the movement to preserve wilderness areas.

Q: *What would be his message to kids?*
A: Enjoy the natural world. Learn from it.

Q: *Why is it important to set aside places such as Sagamore Hill in addition to wilderness areas?*
A: We better understand people's actions when we understand how they lived. It makes history real for us. It's what I call time travel. When you walk into Roosevelt's study and you see his pictures, his desk, and his possessions, you feel a connection. His life and spirit are there.

▼MONUMENTS such as the Statue of Liberty are also run by the National Park Service.

Theodore Roosevelt's
KEY DATES

1858	Born on October 27, in New York City
1897	Named Assistant Secretary of the Navy
1898	Leads Rough Riders in Spanish-American War; elected governor of New York
1900	Elected vice president
1901	McKinley shot; Roosevelt becomes president
1904	Elected president; begins Panama Canal
1906	Wins Nobel Peace Prize
1912	Loses race for the presidency
1919	Dies on January 6, in Oyster Bay, New York

1865 The U.S. Civil War ends.

1903 The Wright brothers fly the first powered airplane.

1909 Explorers Robert E. Peary and Matthew Henson reach the North Pole.